FIRST
BIOGRAPHIES

Johnny Appleseed

Published by Raintree Steck-Vaughn Publishers, an imprint of Steck-Vaughn Company

Planned and produced by The Creative Publishing Company
Editors: Christine Lawrie and Pam Wells

Library of Congress Cataloging-in-Publication Data

Holland, Gini.
    Johnny Appleseed / Gini Holland; illustrated by Kim Palmer.
      p.   cm. — (First biographies)
    Summary: Relates the life and accomplishments of John Chapman.
    ISBN 0-8172-4452-2
    1. Appleseed, Johnny, 1774-1845 — Juvenile literature.   2. Apple growers— United States — Biography — Juvenile literature.   3. Frontier and pioneer life — Middle West — Juvenile literature.   [1. Appleseed, Johnny, 1774-1845.   2. Apple growers.   3. Frontier and pioneer life.]
    I. Palmer, Kim (Kim L.), 1961-   ill.   II. Title.   III. Series.
    SB63.C46H65   1997
    634'.11'092 — dc20   96-7230
    [B]   CIP
                                                        AC

Printed and bound in the United States
1 2 3 4 5 6 7 8 9 0 W 99 98 97 96

FIRST BIOGRAPHIES

Johnny Appleseed

Gini Holland
Illustrated by Kim Palmer

RSVP

RAINTREE
STECK-VAUGHN
PUBLISHERS
The Steck-Vaughn Company

Austin, Texas

The American pioneers called him Johnny Appleseed, but his real name was John Chapman. Johnny was a friend of the pioneers. He helped them make new homes in wild places. He became a legend in his own time. He only worked as far west as Ohio and Indiana, but even pioneers in states farther west said they had seen him.

Stories have a way of changing over time. Maybe that is why the story of Johnny Appleseed became a mix of facts and tall tales over the years. However, one part of the story has always stayed the same. People loved Johnny Appleseed.

Johnny was born on September 26, 1774, two years before the United States was born, on July 4, 1776. In fact, John Chapman was born so long ago that when he was a boy in Massachusetts, people still thought the states of Ohio and Indiana were in "the Far West."

Johnny's life was spent making other people happy, but his own childhood began sadly. His mother and baby brother died before he was two years old. His father was off fighting with George Washington's army in New York at the time. Only his six-year-old sister Elizabeth was there to comfort him. Together they waited for their father to come home.

When Johnny was about five years old, his father married a woman named Lucy Cooley. The children moved to their new stepmother's home in Longmeadow, Massachusetts. Johnny started school there, and learned to read and write well. But he was often a dreamer in class.

Johnny's parents had ten more children. Johnny was a gentle and loving child. He helped care for his new brothers and sisters. He was a big help to his stepmother.

Johnny liked walking alone in the woods. He was soon at home in the forest. It was a great place to learn about animals. And he could always find a quiet place to read his favorite book, the Bible.

When he was a teenager, Johnny walked all the way across New York State. His younger brother Nathaniel went with him. The friendly Seneca and Munsee Indians taught them how to survive, or stay alive, in the forest. Johnny used these skills in his later life.

Then Johnny got a job in an apple orchard. In those days, there were no refrigerators to keep food fresh. But apples could be stored a long time. People could also make apples last longer by making apple cider and apple butter.

Johnny learned all about growing apples. He started
to save the seeds that dropped from the cider press.
The Bible and his Indian friends had taught him not
to waste anything. The cider press owner didn't want
the seeds. Johnny knew they contained the makings
of an apple tree. He saw how valuable the seeds were.

Johnny knew people were traveling west to find land to farm. He went west ahead of these pioneers and cut down parts of the forests to plant apple orchards. Then he sold the young trees and fresh apples to settlers as they came.

He had many orchards, so he had a good
business. He spent a lot of time traveling from
orchard to orchard to care for his trees. He pruned
the trees carefully and built brush fences around
the orchards.

Johnny Chapman was not the first to bring apple trees west. The French brought them as far west as the Great Lakes and Mississippi Valley. His gift to settlers was to plant the trees before the families arrived. When they got there, Johnny was ready to sell, trade, and give seeds away.

Map of North America in about 1800

In those days, there were no telephones, radios, or televisions. John Chapman spread the news. As he traveled he also shared tales of adventure, Bible stories, and love along with his apple seeds.

Sadly, the new towns and farms of the settlers destroyed Indian hunting grounds. The Indians began to fight back. Some tribes joined the British in the War of 1812. Most Indian tribes knew Johnny as a friend. This meant he could travel through their territory. He was able to warn settlers when Indians and the British were going to attack the settlements.

Sometimes even Johnny was chased by angry Indians. He would hide rather than fight. Johnny did not believe in killing. He would not even kill animals for meat. Sometimes he lived on nuts during harsh winters, rather than kill any animal for food.

Johnny was always willing to lend a hand to settlers. He helped them with their barn raising and fence building, so he was welcome wherever he went.

Settlers were hungry for more than apples. They wanted Johnny's company and his news of the places he had come from. Everyone loved to hear his stories. A visit from Johnny Appleseed was a special treat for young and old alike.

By 1824, Johnny's chosen life was to live in the woods and make overnight stays at settlers' homes. He was very religious and tried to live like the early Christians. He even went barefoot. Some people said this was to punish his feet for stepping on a snake by mistake.

He dressed strangely and lived in such an unusual way that tall tales got mixed up with real stories about him, even during his lifetime. His homemade hats and sackcloth shirts looked very funny. People said he carried his "mush-pot" on his head for a hat. Maybe, once or twice, he did.

The legend of Johnny Appleseed often went ahead of him. There were true stories of his kindness to all creatures. One time, a bee got stuck in his pant leg. He gently set it free even though it stung him on its way out. Other stories may have been made up. People told about his playing with bear cubs beside a friendly mama bear.

He really was known for walking in his bare feet. Some people said his feet were too tough to be cut by rattlesnake fangs! They even said he could walk for miles on ice. At least once he actually floated down a river using a cake of ice for a boat.

Settlers who knew Johnny wrote down some of these stories. They wrote about how strong he was. He could chop down twice as many trees in one day as any other man. If anyone wanted to pick a fight with him, he would have a chopping contest instead. This meant he always won!

Johnny was kind to people and animals. He bought animals that were too old to work and gave them to people who would look after them.

Sadly, at age 71, old age caught up with Johnny. He was not strong enough to survive his rugged way of life. He caught pneumonia while walking through a snowstorm in Indiana, and died on March 10, 1845.

When he died, he left apple trees across the Midwest. All the pioneers he had helped remembered his goodness, too. People began to think of him as both a folk hero and a saint. His good heart and unusual ways made him as important as the make-believe Paul Bunyan and Pecos Bill.

But Johnny Appleseed was a real person. He was a man who made a big difference, just by being himself. To this day, school children across the United States still remember him and sing about his life.

Key Dates

1774 Born to Nathaniel and Elizabeth Chapman in Leominster, Massachusetts, on September 26.

1776 His mother dies sometime before he is two years old. (Date unknown).

1779 His father remarries, making Lucy Cooley Johnny's stepmother.

1797 Leaves Massachusetts for northwest Pennsylvania to plant apple trees.

1800 Travels into Ohio.

1812 Warns Ohio settlers of Indian attacks.

1828 Travels as far west as Fort Wayne, Indiana.

1845 Dies near Fort Wayne, Indiana, on March 10.